TOM COCKLE

WAR
PHOTOGRAPHER

peko
PUBLISHING

1.2

INTRODUCTION

This volume is divided into two separate subjects. The first part presents a number of new photographs from the personal photo album of Oberleutnant d.R Peter Prien who began his army career with Pz.Nachr.Abt.37 with 1.Panzer-Division in January 1941 and finished the war as Führer of the Stabskompanie of Pz.Rgt.3 of 2.Panzer-Division. His album contains mostly photos of his time with 2.Panzer-Division around the time of the Kursk battles. (Page 3-39).

The second part presents a series of photographs of the 8.8cm Flak 18 mounted on the chassis of the Sd.Kfz.8 half-track officially known as the 8.8cm Flak 18 Sfl. auf schwere Zugkraftwagen 12 t (Sd.Kfz.8) als Fahrgestell. Most are new and previously unpublished. (Page 40-59).

Peter Prien was born on June 9, 1922 at Altona an der Elbe in Schleswig-Holstein. After graduating from school in 1940, he did his compulsory six-month service in the Reichsarbeitsdienst completing in August whereupon, he entered training with Pz.Nachr.Ers.Abt.37 in September at Erfurt. After completing his training, he was sent to Russia in January 1941, joining Pz.Nachr.Abt.37 with 1.Panzer-Division. In September 1941, he was transferred to Pz.Nachr.Abt.140 of the newly formed 22.Panzer-Division in France. The division was sent to Odessa, Russia in February 1942 and then to the Crimea where it suffered heavy losses. After this, they participated in battles in the Kharkov and Rostov areas. In June 1942, after successfully completing an eight-week course at one of the German military Kriegsschule, Prien was sent to Panzertruppenschule Wünsdorf for a 16-week training course designed to familiarize officer candidates with the workings of a Panzer and the tactics to be used in the field. In October 1942, newly promoted Leutnant d.R. Peter Prien was transferred to 2./Pz.Nachr.Abt.38 from 2.Panzer-Division then fighting in Russia. In August 1943, he was assigned as Nachr.Offz. of Pz.Gren.Rgt.2 and then, after being promoted to Oberleutnant in January 1944, became the Nachr.Offz. of Pz.Rgt.3 in February.

During his career, he received many awards, the Iron Cross First and Second Class, the Ehrenblattspange (Honor Roll Clasp), the Deutsches Kreuz in gold, the Tank Assault Badge, Eastern Front Medal and two Tank Destruction Badges. There is some controversy surrounding his award of the Knights Cross in 1945. He was recommended for the Knights Cross on 28 March 1945 however, no documentation could be found to support it. A second mention is made around 9 May 1945 that due to the end of the war would have been illegal. Based on the photographs of Prien smiling and posing with his Knights Cross I tend to believe that the award in March was legitimate. It seems unreasonable that he would be posing for these photos on the day after Germany officially surrendered.

© PeKo Publishing Kft.

Published by
PeKo Publishing Kft.
8360 Keszthely, Bessenyei György utca 37., Hungary
Email: info@pekobooks.com
www.pekobooks.com

Responsible publisher
Péter Kocsis

Author
Tom Cockle

Layout
nadam.hu

Printed in Hungary

Photos
Péter Kocsis

First published
2020

ISBN 978-615-5583-24-7

All rights reserved. No parts of this publication may be reproduced, or transmitted in any form or by any means, electronic or mechanical, including photocopying, recording or by any information storage and retrieval system, without permission from the Publisher in writing.

Above: This dunkelgrau RAL 7021 Auto-Union Horch 901 Typ 40 Kfz.15 radio car in Russia displays the emblem for a vehicle attached to the Nachrichtungzug on the right side. The falling star emblem in a white outlined shield on the left side resembles that of Luftlande-Sturm-Regiment 1 but was used by 2.Panzer-Division from September 1942 until early 1943.

Above left: This le.Pz.Sp.Wg. (Fu) (Sd.Kfz.223) Ausf.B 5.Serie has a new coat of winter whitewash applied over the original dunkelgrau RAL 7021 paint. Of special note is the MG turret has been replaced with an armored shield from an Sd.Kfz.250 or 251. Among other modifications on the Ausf.B 5.Serie, the turn signals were relocated to the front fenders and the fire extinguisher mounted on the right rear fender. Brackets were added on each side at the rear for stowing a Sternantenne a and four 1.25 m Steckmast.

Left: A Marder 38t Ausf.H, probably from Pz.Jg.Abt.38 from 2.Panzer-Division, rolls through a Russian village. The first four of these vehicles were delivered to the unit in early December 1942 so this photo is likely taken in the early spring of 1943. In the background is a later model Auto-Union Horch 901 Typ 40 Kfz.15 featuring the spare wheel mounted on the outside of the body. Implemented in 1940, it simplified construction and provided more interior space.

A Pz.Fu.Wg. (Sd.Kfz.263) (8 Rad) 1.Serie from Pz.Nachr.Abt.38 of 2.Panzer-Division seen in Russia in 1942. It has a light color camouflage pattern sprayed over its original dunkelgrau RAL 7021 paint. There were 100 built on the 1.Serie GS Fahrgestell from 1937 until 1939.

5

The same armored car has become bogged down in a muddy Russian field. Tow cables can be seen attached to the rear to help pull the vehicle out. The 9 m telescoping Kurbelmast 'P' is covered with a protective canvas tarp.

Above right: This kl.Pz.Fu.Wg. (Sd.Kfz.260) Ausf.B 5.Serie also has a carefully applied coat of winter whitewash paint applied to it. They were equipped with a Fu 7 with a 20W sender 'd' and Ukw.E.'d1' receiver operating in the same frequency as aircraft along with a Fu.Spr. Ger. 'a'. The standard 2 m rod antenna is mounted to the roof. The forward bracket for the Sternantenne and Steckmast can be seen above the jack base.

Above left: An infantry Leutnant and an assistant gaze out from the cramped confines of their kl.Pz.Fu.Wg. (Sd.Kfz.260). It appears that a table was installed the full width of the compartment to provide a place to spread out maps and books required for their duty. Details of the wire mesh anti-grenade screens can be clearly seen in this view.

Right: The same infantry Leutnant and a Panzer Leutnant discuss the situation at a temporary table while another Panzer officer looks on. The medal pinned to his tunic is the War Merit Cross First Class with Swords awarded to soldiers for exceptional service not in direct connection with combat.

7

This Pz.Kpfw.II Ausf.J (Sd.Kfz.121) likely belonged to 12.Pz.Div. which was issued with ten in late December 1942 after being transferred to the Roslavl area in central Russia. Originally conceived in 1939 as a heavy reconnaissance tank, it had 80mm armor plates on the front and 50mm on the sides and rear. Armed with a 2cm Kw.K38 and an MG34, only 30 were ever completed.

Weighing 19t, it was designed with five interleaving road wheels on torsion bars with 500mm wide tracks to reduce the ground pressure. A large round hatch was provided on each side for the two crewmen, which required a section of the fenders to be left open. The commander was provided with the same cupola with periscopes designed for the Pz.Kpfw.II Ausf.F.

An almost new m.Kdo.Pz.Wg. (Sd.Kfz.251/6) Ausf.C is parked beside the road. Fitted with a prominent frame antenna, the vehicle was originally fitted with one Fu 12 80W and one Fu19 15W radio set. A battalion command pennant, pink with a black stripe, is mounted on the left fender.

Above top: A close up photo of this Panzer Oberleutnant shows the details of the silver braid on his black M1938 officer's quality Feldmütze with the inverted 'V' soutache of rose pink Waffenfarbe over the national cockade in silver bullion on black and red cloth boss.

Above bottom: The next series of photos shows group of officers assembled in a field for target practice. The nearest officer is wearing the Panzer uniform and the twisted braid on his shoulder straps indicate a rank of at least a Major. He is wearing his field grey M1938 Feldmütze. The other officers are wearing the M1936 service tunic with dark blue-green collar. The closest is wearing the ribbon of the Iron Cross Second class in the second buttonhole of his tunic. Note the ammunition clip in his hand.

Above left: This Panzer Leutnant is lying in position on the ground with a standard issue 7.92mm Kar98K rifle in his hands. His black M1938 Feldmütze has the white on black BeVo woven eagle and a woven cockade.

Right: Here we see the Major assuming his firing position on the ground.

Above: Three soldiers pose for a photo at a lager somewhere in Russia during the early summer of 1943. The closest one is a Feldwebel who is wearing an M1936 service tunic with the blue-green collar and a First Class Marksmanship Lanyard on his right shoulder. It may be a Fifth Class lanyard but it is difficult to tell if it has the crossed swords in front of the shield. He is also wearing riding breeches, with less pronounced cloth doubling on the insides of the legs and seat, and marching boots instead of riding boots with spurs.

Above left: Four other soldiers pose for their photo, probably at the same location. The Feldwebel at the left also wears riding breeches with marching boots. His M1940 tunic no longer has the blue-green collar but retains the pleated pockets and three-point flap. It has the double row of braid around the lower sleeve indicating his position as 'der Spiess', (regimental Sargent-Major), usually with the rank of Hauptfeldwebel.

Left: The group of officers has gathered around to chat during the exercise as each waits his turn with the rifle. On the left, an enlisted man watches with binoculars to report the results of each shot.

Three photos of a Pz.Kpfw.II Ausf.B that has been modified by adding 20mm plates to the front of the turret and superstructure. Additionally, a new commander's cupola with periscopes was added. A 15mm plate with a cutout for the driver's hatch was added above the existing curved glacis and a 20mm plate added to the front of the lower hull. A large stowage bin was added to the right fender. The tactical emblem painted on the front plate and damaged stowage bin indicates it is assigned to 3./Pz.Pi.Btl.38.

A wooden crate is stowed on the engine deck with the old German phrase, 'Nicht Ärgern! Nur Wundern!' (Don't be annoyed, just wonder) in white gothic script. The tactical emblem has been repeated on the side of the hull. We can also see that the vehicle has had the long cylindrical muffler replaced with a shorter flattened one from a Pz.Kpfw.II Ausf.F.

A Pz.Bef.Wg. Tiger Ausf.E from s.Pz.Abt.505 seen in the late spring of 1943. It is fitted with smoke dischargers on the turret, 'S' mine launchers on the hull, the early Feifel air filters and a wide storage bin with parallel sides and a cutout for the escape hatch. These features indicate it was probably one of the first of three built in February 1943. Note the initial location of the Sternantenne stowage tube on the side of the hull under the standard antenna stowage tube.

The same battalion headquarters Pz.Bef.Wg. Tiger Ausf.E with a newly painted Roman numeral 'II' on the turret. The charging buffalo emblem of the battalion can be faintly seen painted on the front plate to the right side, as viewed, of the driver's visor. The battalion headquarters was equipped with two Befehlstiger and one Pz.Kpfw.III Ausf.M.

Here we get a better view of the Sternantenne stowage tube mounted on the side of the hull and we can also see the plug welded into the aperture in the mantlet for the coaxial machine gun. Just to the right of the tree the lower support bracket for the Steckmast can be seen. It appears to have been painted in a three-color camouflage scheme of rotbraun RAL 8017 and olivgrün RAL 6003 over the dunkelgelb RAL 7028 base color.

Above left: Three crew members of the Pz.Bef.Wg. Tiger Ausf.E pose for a photo on the front of their vehicle. The K.F.F.2 twin driver's periscope was dropped starting in February 1943 and the holes plugged and welded shut.
Above: Another view of the Pz.Bef.Wg. Tiger Ausf.E hidden in the trees to conceal it from enemy aircraft during the build up to Operation 'Zitadelle'.

The Pz.Bef.Wg. Tiger Ausf.E some time later is moving out in preparation for the upcoming battle. The battalion fielded a full complement of 45 Tigers at the beginning of Operation 'Zitadelle', the last 14 from 3.Kompanie arriving on 19 June 1943, replacing all their Pz.Kpfw.III.

Another view of the Pz.Bef.Wg. Tiger Ausf.E from a different vantage point with all of the crew aboard. The charging bull emblem has been painted out leaving a large contrasting patch on the front plate. The long pry bar normally carried on the hull roof beside the turret has been placed in the shovel brackets on the glacis plate.

Having only been in service for about three months, the Tiger is still in almost new condition. In this photo and the previous two, it appears that the camouflage paint scheme has been altered from that seen in the first photos.

A new looking Tiger Ausf.E from s.Pz.Abt.505 just before Operation 'Zitadelle'. Although the bright sunlight has washed out the contrast in the colors, it also appears to have been painted in a three-color camouflage scheme of rotbraun RAL 8017 and olivgrün RAL 6003 over the dunkelgelb RAL 7028 base color with the number '131' painted in red with a white outline. The S-mine discharger on the right rear side and standard turret stowage bin indicate this Tiger was produced in January 1943.

A group of soldiers, including the crew of this Auto-Union Horch 901 Typ 40 Kfz.17 Fu.Kw. (radio car) look over a Messerschmitt Bf 109 that has had a mishap landing when the right landing gear collapsed. The apparatus on the front and back of the roof on the Horch were used to raise and lower the frame antenna, which is missing here.

Above: A Borgward BIV from Panzer-Kompanie (Fkl) 312 which was assigned to clear paths through minefields for the advancing Tigers of s.Pz.Abt.505 at the beginning of Operation Zitadelle. Although fitted with the later metal tracks, the location of the antenna behind the driver indicates that this is an Ausf.A production vehicle. They carried a 450kg explosive charge. A total of 628 Ausf.A were built from April 1942 to June 1943.

Left: Panzer-Kompanie (Fkl) 312 used the StuG.III Ausf.G as a command tank to control the Borward BIV demolition vehicles. The unit was equipped with seven StuG.III Ausf.G and twenty-four Borgward BIV with another twelve in reserve.

The crewmen of this early Pz.Bef.Wg.III Ausf.H have camouflaged their vehicle with cut foliage to help conceal it from enemy aircraft in the days leading up to Operation Zitadelle. The early versions were characterized by the installation of a dummy 3.7cm gun in a bolted alloy mantlet. The Doppeladler emblem on a white shield with a cross in the center, adopted by the regiment for Operation Zitadelle, can be seen painted on the side of the turret. Six Pz.Bef.Wg. were reported in service at the time.

This Pz.Kpfw.III Ausf.N is one of 167 completed on diverted Pz.Kpfw.III Ausf.M production in 1943. The watertight covers on the engine air intakes can be seen and it is still fitted with the turret mounted smoke dischargers. The Doppeladler emblem is painted on the side of the turret with a white cross in the center. It has been converted to a command vehicle with an additional 2 m antenna mounted on the rear fender. The division was equipped with twenty for Operation Zitadelle.

Another Pz.Bef.Wg.III Ausf.H concealed among the trees at another location nearby. Close examination reveals that a Balkenkreuz has been painted on the side of the turret and the tactical sign for a vehicle attached to the Nachrichtungzug can be faintly seen on the front fender. The 2 m rod antenna has been badly bent.

Above: This is probably the same Pz.Bef.Wg.III Ausf.H as the previous photo with the Balkenkreuz on the turret and the stowage box bolted to the fender. The armored cover that protected the entry point into the turret for the cable from the frame antenna is missing revealing that it was held in place by three bolts and not welded to the turret. The Leutnant in the turret appears to Peter Prien.

Left: In this photo, both men are posing outside the vehicle sitting on the cupola. An additional visor and a pistol port were provided on the right side and a pistol port on the left side of the superstructure on the Pz.Bef.Wg.III Ausf.E and Ausf.H. The supports for the frame antenna are made of wood to prevent the antenna from grounding on the hull.

Right: A close-up view of the turret of a Pz.Bef.Wg.III Ausf.H showing it is welded to a thin plate that is then bolted to the top of the hull. Normally the wooden antenna trough had an extension mounted on top of the toolbox to protect the antenna from being damaged by the crew entering or exiting the turret hatch but it is missing from this vehicle. Note the two pieces of steel tubing welded to the cupola, possibly used for a sunshade.

Above: A mechanic gives a friendly smile for the camera while standing inside the engine bay of a Pz.Bef.Wg.III Ausf.H. A spare track link bracket can be seen mounted to the underside of the open engine deck hatch.

A senior commander, holder of the Knight's Cross, looks out of the turret of his Pz.Bef.Wg.III Ausf.H during the advance with tanks of the division arrayed in the distance. The outer edge of a later cast drive sprocket can be seen although it is still fitted with the early idler. The photographer was probably standing in one of the command half-tracks as evidenced by the section of the frame antenna in the foreground.

This Pz.Kpfw.II Ausf.B has been fitted out as a command vehicle with additional radios and a field modified frame antenna on the engine deck. Additional storage bins have been added to the right fender with space for two spare road wheels. In the background can be seen the Befehlstiger, a Pz.Bef.Wg.III Ausf.H and an Auto-Union Horch 901 Typ 40 Kfz.17 Fu.Kw. on the left.

An Sd.Kfz.251/6 Ausf.C m.Kdo.Pz.Wg. (mittlere Kommandopanzerwagen) with a Balkenkreuz unusually painted on the driver's front plate, is concealed in the trees while on the right is an Sd.Kfz.251/6 Ausf.A, as evidenced by the visor in the superstructure side to the right of the Balkenkreuz. In the foreground is an Sd.Kfz.251/7 Ausf.C m.Pi.Pz.Wg. (mittlere Pionierpanzerwagen) with the number '01' painted on the front plate and side of the engine compartment.

In this photo, the Sd.Kfz.251/7 has moved up in front of the Befehlstiger. It was normally equipped with two 8 t Übergangsschienen, 8 metric-ton portable bridge sections, carried on special brackets on each side of the hull, which have been replaced here by two large wooden planks.

Another view of the Sd.Kfz.251/7 Ausf.C with the number '01' painted on the front, showing the crew climbing aboard as they prepare to move out. To the left is the Sd.Kfz.250/5 Ausf.A where we can see the armored cover around the porcelain mount for the Sternantenne d on the upper rear side of the hull. In the foreground to the left are two Pz.Bef.Wg.III Ausf.H.

Clouds of exhaust fill the air as the march begins. In front are two Pz.Bef.Wg.III Ausf.H still carrying the cut foliage that was used to conceal them from aerial observation. The one on the right is the same one previously seen with the bent antenna and the tactical sign for a Nachrichtung unit painted on the right fender. In the background is Sd.Kfz.251/6 Ausf.C with the Balkenkreuz painted on the driver's front plate.

Pz.Rgt.3 was equipped with 59 Pz.Kpfw.IV Ausf.G at the start of Operation Zitadelle. Both of these late production vehicles have a reinforced cupola with a one-piece hatch introduced in February 1943 and welded 30mm Zusatzpanzer plates on the front of the hull and superstructure. The 7.5cm Kw.K.40 L/48 as seen on the vehicle on the right, replaced the L/43 gun, as seen on the left one and Schürzen (side skirts) began to be installed as a defense against Russian anti-tank rifles in April 1943 as well. Compare the design of the Doppeladler emblem to the previous photos; this one has a colored cross on a white shield.

The same Pz.Kpfw.IV Ausf.G as seen in the previous photo. Note how the angle of sunlight falling on it has washed out the colors of the camouflage paint on the Schürzen and the cross on the white shield. As only II./Pz.Rgt.3 took part in Operation Zitadelle, the white stenciled number on the back of the turret Schürzen could be either '501' or '601'.

Left: This is a head-on view of the same Pz.Kpfw.IV Ausf.G without the Schürzen, seen in the previous photo. The holes in the front plate for the driver's were plugged after the K.F.F.2 twin periscopes were dropped from production in February 1943. We also have a good view of the antenna deflector that was welded to the gun mantlet starting in November 1942.

Bottom: A close-up look into the radio operator's position in a Pz.Kpfw. IV Ausf.G showing us how cramped it is inside the vehicle. He has his headphones on and adjusting the radio while balancing a map board on his lap. Sitting on the front of the superstructure, a Panzergrenadier Unteroffizier wearing a one-piece coverall. Appears to be relaying a written message to the radio operator for transmission. Note the dunkelgrau RAL 7021 paint on the inside of the hatch.

Top: Two Panzergrenadier officers can now be seen to the side of the group in the previous photos. Unfortunately, none of the officers are identifiable.

Right above and bottom: A group of Panzer officers confer with their maps during the advance on Kursk. In the background on the left is an Sd.Kfz.251/1 Ausf.C m.Schützen.Pz.Wg. with a Horch 830 B1 Kfz.15 Fu.Kw. (radio car) in the middle and the rear of a Pz.Kpfw.III on the right. Although the photo is quite blurry, the rear idler appears to be the early eight-hole type perhaps indicating it is a Pz.Bef.Wg.III.

Bottom: The Enigma machine was an encryption device employed by the German military and diplomatic corps during World War II. Invented by the German engineer Arthur Scherbius at the end of World War I, it was patented in 1918 and the first commercial models were marketed in 1923. In this photo, four officers and an NCO appear to be using one to send or receive a message.

Above: Three more officers are looking over their maps prior to or during the battle. Two of them are wearing the waterproof motorcyclists coat, or Kradmantle, that was a very popular and practical garment among officers as well. They were field-grey in color and cut long with tails that could be gathered around the rider's legs for ease of movement while on the motorcycle. The officer in the background is wearing his standard M36 pattern tunic with the blue-green faced collar.

Left and above: Gen.Lt. Dietrich von Saucken, commander of 4.Panzer-Division and Gen. Lt. Vollrath Lübbe, commander of 2.Panzer-Division in conference on the battlefield. Von Saucken is wearing the Knights Cross worn on a ribbon around his neck. He is also wearing the ribbon of the Iron Cross, Second Class from World War I in his buttonhole with the clasp indicating the subsequent award of the Nazi Iron Cross, Second Class.

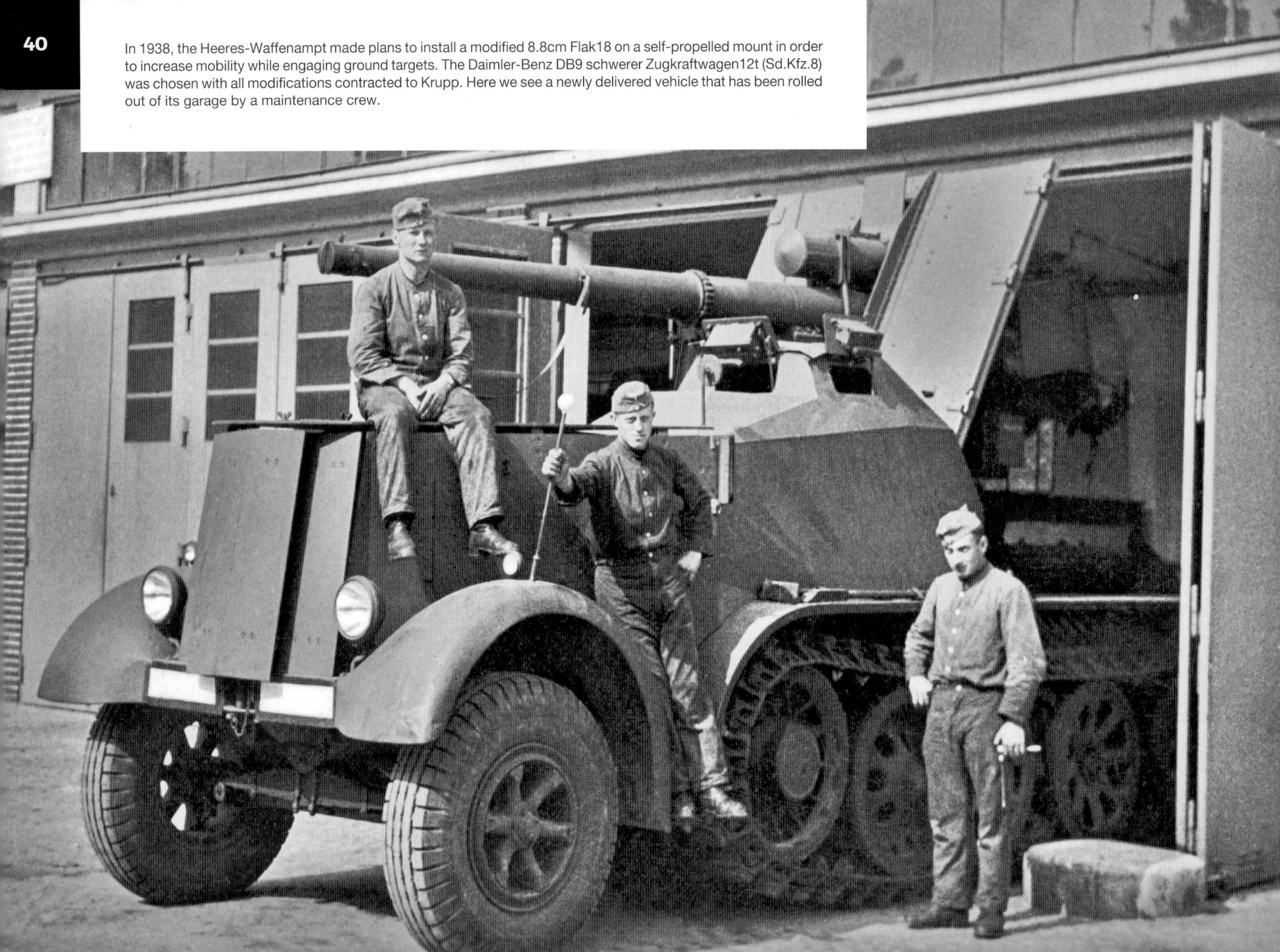

In 1938, the Heeres-Waffenampt made plans to install a modified 8.8cm Flak18 on a self-propelled mount in order to increase mobility while engaging ground targets. The Daimler-Benz DB9 schwerer Zugkraftwagen12t (Sd.Kfz.8) was chosen with all modifications contracted to Krupp. Here we see a newly delivered vehicle that has been rolled out of its garage by a maintenance crew.

In this view of the opposite side, we can see the 14.5mm armor plates installed around the front of the Sd.Kfz.8 to protect the engine and driver's compartment. A 10mm thick armored shield with folding sides was mounted to protect the gun crew and a steel pipe bumper added to chassis extensions on the front.

Three new vehicles are lined up on a parade ground after delivery. One identifying feature of the Sd.Kfz.8 is the eight pie-shaped holes in the outer road wheels. A variety of inner road wheels were installed including these ones with six large round holes hear the hub and twelve smaller holes around the outside.

There are at least eight new vehicles lined up in this photo, which have by now been assigned Wehrmacht vehicle registration numbers. The gun was supplied with both armor piercing and high explosive rounds carried in the 18 round diagonal ammunition stowage bin on the rear.

In this view, we can see a ninth vehicle on the far side of the one covered with a tarp and so the tenth one must be just out of sight in either photo. The presence of the young boys on their bikes indicates the photo was probably taken before the war broke out.

A clear left side view in which we can see the faint outline of the two-color paint scheme of dunkelgrau Nr.46 and dunkelbraun Nr.45. In most black and white photos, the scheme is hard to see due to dust collecting on the vehicles. Note the rear idler has been positioned so it is on the ground, possibly due to the weight of the gun overtaxing the suspension.

All ten guns were issued to 1./Pz.Jg.Abt.8 which saw its first action in Poland in September 1939. In the spring of 1940, it was renamed 1./s.Pz.Jg.Abt.8 with only six guns. They saw action in France in May 1940 with Guderian's XIX.Panzerkorps supporting 1. and 2.Pz.Div. The vehicles have now been fitted with a steel pipe bumper and sheet metal covers on the headlights. A thin white outline Balkenkreuz has been painted on the side of the engine compartment.

Judging from the crewman sitting on the wicker ammunition containers reading the newspaper, this gun is parked at the side of the road somewhere in France in 1940. Since there was no cab access, a different type of drive sprocket hub was utilized. A MAN 3t truck is passing on the left.

The unit lost one gun in at Chémery-sur-Bar about 13km south of Sedan though it is not clear if this was a result of combat. The steel pipe bumper and headlight cover details can be clearly seen as well as the tread plate design on the curved fender in front of the drive sprockets. The white 'K' on the right fender indicates it is attached to Panzergruppe Kleist. The house and shed in the background still exist today at the north end of the village. The man posing for the photo is a civilian official and not a soldier.

Wehrmacht soldiers look over the burned out vehicle, which has settled as the heat from the fire caused the torsion bar suspension to fail. The rubber tires on the road wheels have burned away leaving ash on the ground and the fire has burned the paint on most of the rear of the vehicle and gun. The two trees to the right are both still there today.

This close in view of the fire-blackened rear does not show any evidence of combat damage but looks more like the result of the fuel tank exploding. The location proves the vehicle was headed north towards Sedan and this might have simply been the result of an accidental fire and explosion. The tread plate design can also be seen in the damaged sheet metal deck. Note the two ready rounds of ammunition in the bin on the left side of the breech are still intact.

This photo was taken from a parallel road the led down to the buildings in the background in the previous photo. On this side the fire did not consume the rubber on the road wheels although the suspension has settled. The house on the right also remains today.

Extensive use of chicken wire was used during the French campaign to attach cut foliage in an attempt to conceal the vehicles from the air. Two guns are pulled over to the side of the road while a mechanic attends to an engine problem. The license plates have fairly low numbers painted on, 'WH 1229' and 'WH 5088'. Note the two different styles of drive sprocket hubs.

The same vehicle as in the previous photo, 'WH 5088' is pulled over to the side of the road again with one of the engine compartment covers removed, perhaps indicating another engine problem. The photo also provides a good view of the covered headlights and steel pipe bumper.

In this close-up view we can see numerous clear details of the gun and its mount. The weight of the gun overloaded the chassis by about 2t, which in turn caused additional wear to the suspension. Here, the idler has been removed which also necessitated the removal of the outer road wheel in front of it. There are mounts above the drive sprocket for the gun cleaning rods, 15t jack and a shovel. Note as well the large patch of oil on the ground.

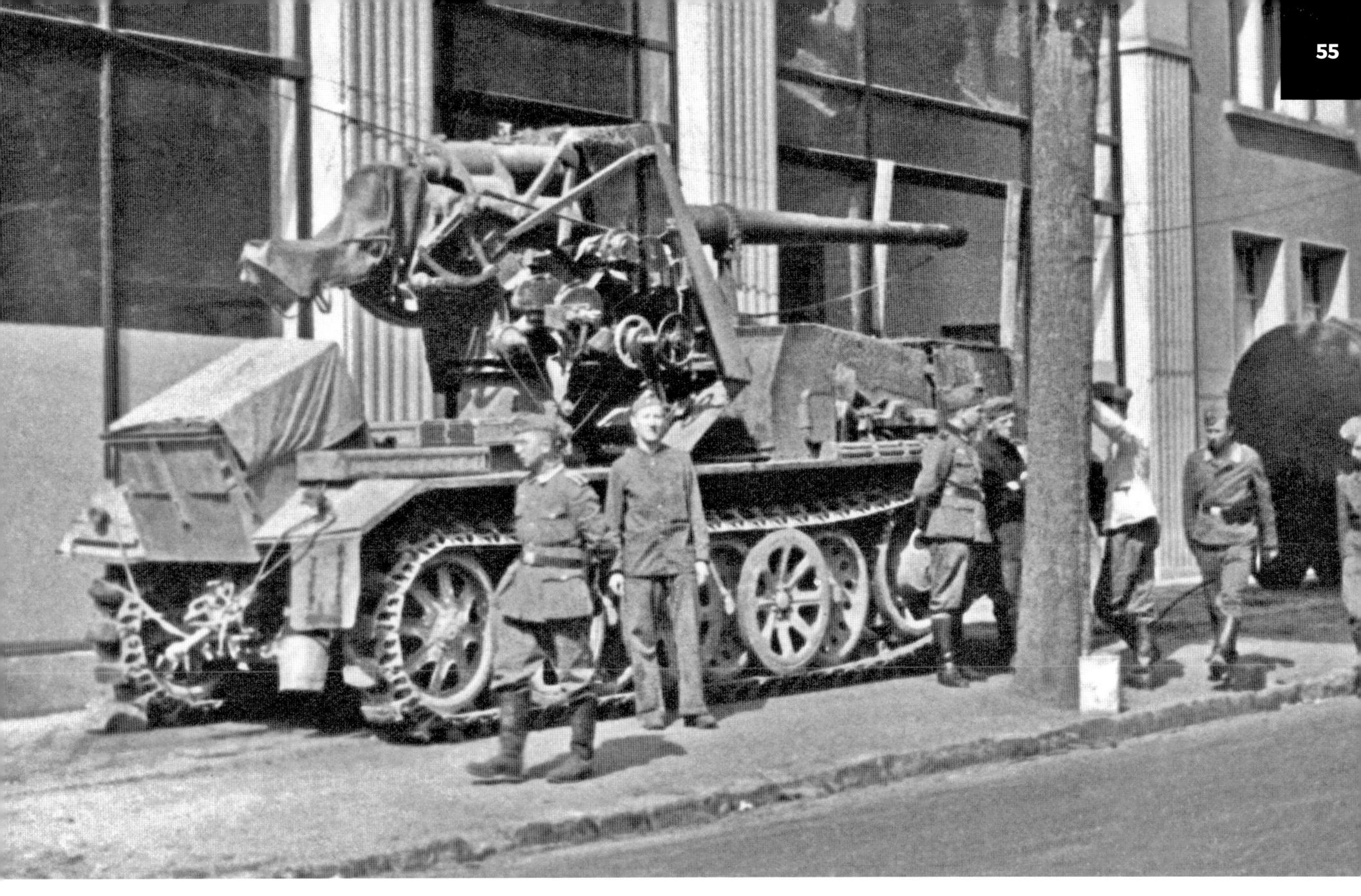

Another gun parked on the sidewalk in a French city, probably to keep the road clear for other traffic. A metal rack has been added on top of the ammunition storage box for additional ammunition storage. On the right two Luftwaffe men casually walk by without seeming to notice anything unusual. Both are wearing the Fliegerbluse that did not have breast pockets. On the left a Wehrmacht Unteroffizier also seems unconcerned with his surroundings.

The weary crewmen of this gun are catching up on some rest beside an open storage shed. Several wicker containers of ammunition are stacked on the back of the vehicle, a common practice. The narrow white outline Balkenkreuz that marked these vehicles during the French Campaign, can be faintly seen on the side of the engine compartment.

The photographer took several photos of this vehicle at this location, many of which have a large number of men in them. Unfortunately, none provide a good view of the license plate number. Except for a few dents in the front fender it seems to have survived the French campaign in good shape. Note the Mercedes three-point star on the drive sprocket hub.

58 The suspension of this vehicle seen in Russia, is very unusual as it employs inside road wheels with four large holes instead of the six holes seen on other early vehicles. The idler is also one of the four-hole wheels when it normally was an eight-spoke wheel that was similar to the outer road wheels. A rack for additional ammunition stowage has been added to the top of the standard bin.

Another heavily camouflaged gun crosses a river on a temporary bridge with the blown remains of the concrete bridge in the background. The emblem painted on the front fender indicates they are attached to Pz.Gr.3 commanded by Gen.Obst. Hermann Hoth. A new style of Balkenkreuz had been adopted with a black center and a thicker white outline. The thin rod with the white ball on top was intended to help drivers know where the front fender was but it doesn't seem to have helped much.

COMING SOON